Discover Your Purpose
WORKBOOK

Table of Contents

Steppingstones to Discover Your Purpose

The purpose of this program is to find the missing pieces of your TRUE story and greater purpose—the one in which you are the hero who turns tragedy into triumph and overcomes the odds—the story that reflects the truth of who you really are. You may not be able to change what happened in the past, but you can change the way you look at your past and change the story you tell about it. Everything might not have been perfect, but everything that has unfolded has provided you with the lessons, the abilities, the tools, and the desires you need to live your destiny.

Your *purpose journey* will help you identify the key pieces of the puzzle that will reveal your life's purpose. Your path to discovery will take you along steppingstones of purpose. Just like steppingstones across a river create a path to get you where you want to go, you will see that these elements from your life all line up to carry you to where you've always been heading.

1) CHILDHOOD INFLUENCES: In this steppingstone, you will examine your childhood influences and the roles you learned to play on the stage of life.
2) PASSIONS AND INTERESTS: In this steppingstone, you will explore what you have been passionate about, both as a child and an adult, as well as how to "find your passion" by developing your interests.
3) TALENTS AND SKILLS: In this steppingstone, you will explore your natural gifts as well as the skills you've acquired over your lifetimes that have uniquely prepared you to reach your potential.
4) PERSONALITY: In this steppingstone, you will explore your natural inclinations, temperament, and preferences to help identify what you are best suited for in your life's purpose.
5) LIFE CHANGING EXPERIENCES: In this steppingstone, you will reflect on the life-changing experiences and turning points that have lead you down your life path.
6) COINCIDENCES: (also referred to as synchronicities)In this steppingstone, , you will identify meaningful coincidences in your life that were pivotal moments that pointedto higher meaning.
7) ELIMINATING LIMITATIONS: In this steppingstone, you will release limiting beliefs and remove any final obstacles from your path.
8) YOUR PURPOSE: In this steppingstone, you will put the pieces together and see what trajectory your steppingstones have created and where they are leading you.
9) MANIFESTO: In this steppingstone, you will create a declaration that expresses your values, beliefs and life purpose in one inspirational, powerful paragraph.
10) LIFE STORY: In this steppingstone, you will rewrite the story you tell, of who you are and what you're on this Earth to do, based on your newfound clarity of how everything in your life has been leading you to be perfectly suited to fulfill your unique purpose.

Let the journey begin!

Conditioning: Childhood Influences

In our society there is a common belief we like to call the "Big Lie"—the idea that our society and childhood upbringing do *not* influence who we are today at the deepest level. Most people don't deny those things have an impact, but they think the effect is minimal and resist believing that their actions and beliefs were formed by other people. However, if we take the time to reflect on how much of what we do and think did not originate as our own idea and let go of things that do not serve us, we are free to embrace beliefs and life choices that genuinely resonate with who we truly are and the life that we want to live. This section is meant to help us reflect on our influences, so we are able to peel away layers of inauthentic belief systems (b.s.) and roles that do not serve us. Remember changing these roles may be challenging because even if they hold us back from our true self, they provide a sense of comfort. This is important to keep in mind because to break a pattern we must be able to remember the bigger picture of why we want to change it. By having a strong enough reason to change and being able to imagine a life that is true to our purpose, we start creating a different reality that will grow and blossom with time.

Answer the questions below. And be sure to take your time. If you need more space, then take out a journal or other materials so you can explore this further. Remember that this is about you and the deeper you can go, reflecting on each area, the better quality of change you will find.

Roles/Conditioning

What roles do you play on the stage of life?

For each role, where did you learn to play the role, or, who told you (or modeled) how to play the role?

How would these roles need to look in order for you to feel that you're living in alignment with your true self?

Who, if anyone, would be affected by you letting go of (or change) the roles that don't serve you?

What benefit do you get from maintaining these roles the way they are?

What benefits would you get from removing or changing these roles?

Who do you think you would be if the roles you don't want to play anymore were to disappear?

Influences on Worldview

Write down words that represent all your caretakers' (any older individual who cared for you or influenced you) beliefs about life (meaning, roles, political, passions or religious beliefs, etc.).

- Circle any beliefs that you have taken on as your own.
- Put a star next to those beliefs you have purposefully NOT adopted.

Take a moment to consider where your caretakers differed from each other on their views of life. Ask yourself if or how you have accommodated both viewpoints and developed your own beliefs somewhere in between.

For each major caretaker, ask yourself what you would say their life "purpose" or mission may have been. What were they passionate about? What did they seem to be trying to accomplish in the world?

Now, ask yourself in what way the missions of your caretakers inspired your current ambitions and values? Did you feel drawn to grab their torch and carry the flame? Or did you feel the need to snuff theirs out and ignite a new, brighter fire?

Stop Trying to "Discover Your Passion"!

Passion is not something that you have to find, it is something you DEVELOP.

6 Characteristics of Passion Development

1. **Passion often develops accidentally.** It begins as an interest or inclination. You have an unintended experience that triggers intrigue, whether it's a science fair experiment in elementary school, a guest speaker in high school, or an enthusiastic college professor who made an otherwise uninteresting topic suddenly appealing. Once this interest is triggered, you follow the impulse and look into it. Sometimes the interest quickly fades and other times you continue to seek to learn more or to experience it again.
2. **Passion takes encouragement and exposure.** In most cases, the initial encounter with the object of interest isn't enough to seal the deal of passion. It takes multiple events and experiences that retrigger the interest over time. Having a mentor or parent encourage further exploration or future exposure is often the catalyst needed to anchor a stronger interest in the topic.
3. **Passion isn't always enjoyable.** Passion begins by following interests that are intrinsically enjoyable. You continue to follow an interest because you enjoy what you're doing. However, as your interest begins to develop into a passion and you get more involved, it becomes more challenging. There may even be aspects of this activity that you don't like or that feel like a chore. But as the level of passion develops, the benefits outweigh the costs.
4. **Passion doesn't require talent or skill, at first.** When we are first beginning anything, it starts out as something we're NOT good at. Passion has to start with play—a willingness to explore for curiosity's sake, not for the reward of being good at it. This is one of the things that holds people back from developing their passion—they're unwilling to do something they're bad at. Even in the situations where some level of natural ability may be required, true skill and talent are developed over time.
5. **Passion takes practice.** For proficiency to develop, which invites a deeper level of exploration and further develops passion, time and effort must be applied. For an interest to develop into a passion, the knowledge or activity have to become second nature. A skill or expertise must be developed. This new ability allows the activity to reach a higher level of enjoyment, when it leads to a state of flow. And to reach this level of mastery, it takes deliberate practice. Not simply exposure or repetition, but commitment to improving through time spent dedicated to the endeavor.
6. **Purpose amplifies passion.** When passion is directed toward a higher purpose, a higher level of meaning and fulfillment can be achieved. Purpose is the conviction that what you are doing matters because it's connected to the wellbeing of others. When you can see the impact your passionate efforts make, you feel even more strongly about what you do.

So, what do you do if you don't have a fully developed passion?

1. **First, let yourself off the hook.** Recognize that a life spent moderately pursuing varied interests will not lead to a clearly identifiable passion, and that's okay. Stop trying to force it. It's never too late to pursue your interests. Having a single, high-intensity passion is not a requirement for a fulfilling life.

2. **Second, begin with what you DO know.** Even if your interests and inclinations are not fully delevloped, follow the trail. Deep down, you know certain things you have NO interest in and others that you do. Allow yourself to explore and play.
3. **Third, be open to trial and error.** Don't be afraid to guess if you're not sure. There isn't just one thing you can become passionate about. And don't be afraid to stop pursuing any interests that lose their appeal. Trying many things, even more than once, is how interests are identified and developed.

And lastly, consider if any of the characteristics of passion development have been holding you back.

1. Have you allowed yourself to follow your impulses or interests? Or do you brush them off as unimportant?

2. Have you put yourself in situations where you could have more exposure to your interests or get more support? Or do you live within the bounds of your comfort zone?

3. Have you allowed yourself to move forward, even in the face of the unpleasant aspects of your interest? Or have you expected perfection and rejected hard work or necessary effort?

4. Have you allowed yourself to play and fail? Or have you avoided your interests because you aren't great at them?

5. Have you applied yourself to deeper exploration through deliberate practice? Or have you left the development of your passion up to chance or follow it only "when I feel like it"?

6. Have you considered the impact you would like to make in the lives of others and the meaning this would bring to your pursuit?

Passions/Interests

In life, there are things we just absolutely *love* to do! There are things we *naturally* feel drawn to. There are activities we lose ourselves in—getting in the *flow*. There are things we're *passionate* about, that inspire us, or that get us all riled up. In a search for your purpose, an important place to look is at THESE things! Purpose implies meaning, yet it also implies something that feels like we were *made* to do. The good news is we instinctually or intuitively know what we're "made for"—we can feel it. It's that inner nudge that pulls us toward what we love, do naturally, and are passionate about.

There are six key elements to igniting your passions by both remembering them and living in alignment with them: childhood wonder, adult passions, your gifts, your dreams, your values, and your commitment.

CHILDHOOD WONDER: Insights from Childhood

You can glean powerful insights into your true nature and natural interests and passions by reflecting on what you were inspired by as a child. Your childhood wonders existed before you developed filters due to the influence of others and the limiting beliefs you developed as you grew up. Often your natural talents, inclinations and interests were lost along the way because you were told they were not practical, realistic, or worthy. Often, you were not even given the chance to explore them through free play and self-directed time. But not all is lost! The true you, your inner child, has always known.

Sometimes our childhood passions and pleasures can bring new life into our adult world. Other times those old inspirations no longer do anything for us and show us how much we've changed.

When I was a child, I wanted to do this when I grew up:

In the past (and as a child), I enjoyed: (Write everything you can think of from food to activities, places you've gone to traditions you've had – list what you liked and WHY you liked it.)

YOUR PASSION: What Do You Love?

Now that you have an idea of what you used to love, it's time to add to your list by looking at your current inspirations.

The activities I do currently that bring me pleasure include:

The activities I know I love that I may not currently be doing but would like to do, include:

The other aspects of life that bring me joy, excitement and that energize me are:

```
[                                                                    ]
[                                                                    ]
[                                                                    ]
[                                                                    ]
```

In my life I have been passionate about:

```
[                                                                    ]
[                                                                    ]
[                                                                    ]
[                                                                    ]
```

These childhood and adult passions and interests are powerful sources of inspiration and fuel for feeding yourself and living with purpose!

YOUR GIFTS: What Do You Have to Offer?

You feel the most alive and passionate about life when you are doing what you are MADE FOR. When you do something that comes naturally to you—a talent—you are fully expressing yourself. Examining your talents and other qualities you have to offer, sheds light on what aspects of yourself you can do the most good with, which also happen to be the same gifts that bring purpose to life.

My best qualities are:

(Ideas)

Humorous	enthusiastic	comforting	determined	intelligent	gentle
Kind	courageous	direct	inspiring	supportive	optimistic
Visionary	compassionate	flexible	entertaining	knowledgeable	
Practical	open generous	strong	energetic	calm	adventurous
Persuasive	patient	insightful	spontaneous	quick-thinking	original

OTHER _____

I am most myself when:

```
[                                                                    ]
[                                                                    ]
[                                                                    ]
[                                                                    ]
```

What makes me feel in flow?

```
[                                                                    ]
[                                                                    ]
[                                                                    ]
[                                                                    ]
```

What comes easy for me that may be hard for others?

```
[                                                                    ]
[                                                                    ]
[                                                                    ]
[                                                                    ]
```

YOUR DREAMS: What Do You Really Want?

Your dreams are calling you. The true you, already knows what they are and never stops dreaming. Often the key to unlocking both your passion and your purpose is to allow yourself to remember your dreams and go for them!

If I could have anything I want, what would it be?

If I could do anything I want, what would it be?

YOUR VALUES: What Do You Stand For?

Sometimes your passions are things that boil your blood. They tug at your heart strings because you care about them. Based on your values and ideals about life you end up wanting the world to be better, often in specific ways. Tuning in to these greater values can unleash your passion.

What would I like to change in the world?

In what way can I BE the change I want to see in the world?

What do I stand for?

YOUR COMMITMENT: How Can I Live in Integrity?

The aspects of my life I am committed to:

The values, dreams, gifts, and passions I am committed to fulfilling in my life:

What it would take for me to be living in integrity:

Talents/Skills

All of us have a multitude of talents and skills, but that does not mean that we are supposed to use them all to follow our purpose. In fact, just because we are good at something does not mean we have to do it or that it will bring us joy. For example, I may be good at data entry, but does that mean that it is part of my purpose? Well, it depends if I feel alive while doing it and it brings me true joy. However, if it does not bring me joy, should I spend my time doing it? Probably not. There's more to purpose than joy. It may be that this particular skill was or will be useful at some point, and it may help me along my path to my purpose. At the same time, there may be things you are good at that you enjoy that are not part of your greater purpose... they may just be something that you enjoy, and that's okay.

Sometimes, we have a talent or skill that we fail to notice because it seems so normal to us that we do not see, that for others, it does not come as natural. For example, we were having a conversation with a colleague who had an amazing talent to bring people together. It seemed that when she wanted to do something at the last minute, she would reach out and quickly have over forty people joining her. After we talked to her about our observation of this phenomena, she remembered that since she was young, she liked doing things in groups. She realized that it came naturally to just reach out to people and coordinate events. However, she had never considered that it was a talent. Through further reflection, she was able to see the power within this ability. She realized she could follow her passion and purpose of bringing people together, and at the same time monetize it.

In this section we will ask you to reflect on your own talents and skills, and will dig deep on what *truly* comes natural to you. For part of this you may want to solicit the help of people around you because they may be able to point out things that you may have not have realized before. One thing that you can do is do a survey with family members, friends, and coworkers (those that are truly supportive) and ask them to tell you at least three things that they consider to be your talents or skills, whether big or small. Let them know that even if it is something that they think you already know, you would appreciate the confirmation via feedback. This is important because they may be reluctant to say things that may seem obvious to them, but they may not be obvious to you.

My key talents/abilities that come naturally to me are: (What do you excel at or do effortlessly?)

I shine when:

I keep being drawn to:

Others tell me I'm good at:

What skills do you have that are unique?

What skills have you acquired that you have found were more useful than you had anticipated?

What talents do you have that come easy to you, which others might find difficult?

Personality

Getting to know yourself through personality assessments can be a fun and insightful process that can lead to greater clarity about what you enjoy and are good at and WHY. It's a useful tool for finding a career that is meaningful and fulfilling, as well as identifying how you and your family, friends or co-workers differ in personality and, therefore, how to improve your relationships. Plus, understanding your personality type might help you gain more clarity about your purpose!

There are many "personality profiles" or tests available. While any quiz can be fun, if you want deeper level insights that are backed up by decades of research and validation, there are several well respected, widely used, and scientifically studied personality profile tests that we recommend. The most famous and widely used is called the Myers Briggs Type Inventory (MBTI). Other popular personality profiles include the DISC (Dominence/Influence/Steadiness/Conscientiosness) and Enneagram tests.

These tests are copyrighted and cannot be shared within this workbook. However, you can take these tests online and use the insights you learn about yourself to aid you in your quest to understand yourself and identify your life's purpose.

Life Changing Experience

Life Timeline

Life is so complex that we sometimes miss patterns or circumstances that have influenced us because we are so focused on getting by or thinking about the past or future. So, what does this mean to you and your purpose? It means that you probably don't remember most of what has influenced you because after it happened you just went back to focusing on living your life, while remembering only the bits that pop up to the surface. Unfortunately, things you've missed are often affecting you today, without your awareness. This is often referred to as the "unconscious mind".

By looking at your life on a timeline you can see it more objectively. You may notice a pattern or a series of experiences that led you toward where you are today. Understanding this, you may notice your life has been leading you towards something. For example, have you ever watched a movie and knew what was going to happen before it happened? If you have, then think of your life in the same perspective. If you can observe the plot of the story, you may be able to decipher where it's going. While reflecting on the experiences of your life, if your first thoughts of the future are negative or limiting it is important to note that you can change and create what you want in life by finding a greater purpose in the experiences. Once something that was unconscious becomes *conscious*, you have *choice*.

Starting at birth, make a list of all significant events that occurred until the present:

Now you are going to summarize your list. Simplify events that are similar. For example, if you moved several times from birth to 16, sum up the experiences by saying "0-16, many moves, learned to be adaptable..." Other summarized statements could be "17-20, turned to academic achievement, discovered I like Science." "20-25, felt lost, kept trying new things."

5-16 _____

17-21 _____

22-30 _____

31-40 _____

41-50 _____
(add additional lines as needed)

What were your turning points?

Do you see any patterns?

What lessons were you taught?

What feels completed for you? Or feel unfinished?

What things energized you?

How have your values changed based on these observations?

What does it look like you've been "in training" for?

What in your life do you see as being heavily focused on?

What stands out?

Coincidences

What is a Coincidence?

Beyond the three-dimensional world of cause and effect, coincidences, often referred to as synchronicities, give us the experience of that which is beyond that cause and effect world. These events are totally unrelated; however, they align in special, unexpected, unexplainable ways beyond what can be rationalized. When people experience a coincidence, they are often left in awe, recognizing that this is no "mere coincidence"—some greater meaning or purpose is behind the seemingly random alignment. Looking back at your timeline, you may see some of those events and recall how they came to be through "coincidental" ways.

Perhaps you've had a friend tell you about a new book and then accidentally knocked a book off the shelf at the store the next day only to realize it's the same book your friend recommended the day before. Maybe you've thumbed through a photo album and saw a photo of an old friend and then received a phone call from him or her that same day. If you can relate to these types of circumstances, you've experienced the phenomenon referred to as coincidence or synchronicity.

The term "synchronicity" was first used by one of the most influential psychologists of all time, Carl Jung. Synchronicity or "coincidence" was one of Jung's most profound contributions to the field of psychology, yet often not well understood. He saw synchronicity as happening beyond the rational mind or even beyond rational expectations in everyday life. He spent 20 years contemplating this phenomenon before publishing his insights about it. So, it's no surprise that not everyone feels drawn to discuss this topic, and that is okay. If you feel inspired by the idea that things coinciding in mysterious ways, beyond what seems rational by "chance" alone, then synchronicities are a great source of meaning for you. If you do not feel that this part of the process is helpful for you, skip it.

Jung shared a famous story about an experience he had with one of his patients, in order to illustrate what he meant by synchronicity. His patient was having a hard time getting out of her head, being wrapped-up in what he referred to as "the self-created prison of her own mind." He realized that using logic would not be able to help this woman. In Jung's words, "I had to confine myself to the hope that something unexpected and irrational would turn up, something that would burst the intellectual retort in which she had sealed herself." She shared with him about a dream she had the previous night, in which someone offered her piece of jewelry containing a golden scarab beetle. As she told the story, they heard a tapping at the window. Jung opened the window and in flew a scarab beetle. He caught the beetle and handed it to her telling her, "Here is your scarab."

Coincidences can contain messages:

Just like a phone message from your dry cleaner doesn't have the same importance as a phone message from your partner, there are different levels of meaning contained within synchronistic messages. Sometimes you have an experience, and you just KNOW it's a clear sign. Other occurrences seem obviously aligned but do not contain any clear meaning.

Follow these steps the next time you experience a synchronicity:

- Become still. Take note of how you are feeling.
- Let your mind wander by relaxing your thoughts so you can tune into your intuition.
- Ask yourself, "What questions have I been asking lately?"
- Consider whether the experience seems connected to another area of your life.
- Observe whether you feel energized.
- If you continue running into someone or continue making eye contact, follow through and start a conversation with that individual.
- When in conversation, follow your intuition if you feel tugged to say something.

- Consider whether there may be something you are able to offer the other person (the synchronistic meaning may be more for him or her than you).
- After the event has passed, reflect on its potential meaning without over-analyzing. Often the subtle meaning is picked up only at the unconscious level.

Not all coincidental experiences are going to be profound, "aha" moments. Most synchronicities are gentle nudges that indicate you are on the right path. As with all things in life, the more you focus on the meaning in life and appreciate the synchronicity, the more you will attract, notice, and experience these tiny miracles!

Synchronicities can hold the secrets that unlock the mystery of our ultimate purpose in life.

Looking back at the trajectory of your life, you may find that synchronistic occurrences have led you to where you are today. Often, we experience unexpected events that are pivotal. Whether we view them as positive or negative, these life-changing experiences are almost always synchronistic. Think back over your life and list any events that occurred that fit into the following descriptions:

- Just at the very moment that I needed _____, _____ happened.
- If I hadn't _____, then _____ this would never have happened.
- Even though _____ was hard, I see now how it was exactly what I needed.
- I can see how _____ happening to me prepared me for _____.
- I wouldn't be who I am or where I am today if it wasn't for _____.
- I was so sure I wanted _____, but when I didn't get it, I realized how it led me to something even better.
- If _____ hadn't gone wrong, I never would have met _____ and _____ never would have happened.

Consider major decisions, events or changes that have occurred in your life. Make note of any unexpected changes or any coincidences that influenced your decisions.

HOME: Were there any particular coincidences or signs connected with getting your current living space? (house numbers, encounters with neighbors, delays, mix-ups, street names, etc.)

JOB: How did you get your present job? (How you found out, who you talked to, what messages you received.)

```
[blank response box]
```

RELATIONSHIP: Describe how you met your most important relationship. What led up to your being in that place at that time?

```
[blank response box]
```

- Are there any obvious synchronicities?
- What does it all seem to be pointing you toward?
- Can you see the direction it may be heading?
- Is there anything that people regularly "tell you" you'd be good at?
- Is there anything you've said along the lines of, "I would love to do _____" but never followed the desire?

Below is a wonderful example of a woman whose synchronistic life experiences led her to her purposeful path. In the 1980s Mary Lee tried convincing her professors to let her create her own "holistic medicine" degree and was told there would be no future in it. (Ha!) Today, she is the founder of Earth Tribe, a successful essential oil company, and she is living in alignment with her true purpose. Mary Lee experienced four major life events that led her to her purpose.

1. As a child, her mother and grandmother used medicines of the earth.
2. She experienced a gas fire and received second-degree burns all over her body and face, which she healed using the essential oil of lavender.
3. She had twin boys and used essential oils during pregnancy, inspiring her to want to share this unknown modality with other pregnant women.
4. She wrote about essential oils in Woman's Day magazine and received hundreds of envelops from women wanting to know more. Her husband said to her, "You should probably start doing this as a business. If you just sit in your room no one will hear your message." And so, she did!

Meaning evolves along every step of our path if we remain open to the subtle guidance that is being offered! Synchronicities are our reminder to experience the joy in daily life and our confirmation that we are on the journey of our greatest purpose.

Be alert with wonder. You never know where your next inspiration is coming from!

Eliminating Limits

We all have limiting beliefs, whether they were created by our selves, people around us, or society. The most impactful thing that you can do is to really look at the BS (belief systems). If you look hard enough, you will find that there is evidence that will contradict that BS. Once you find something that contradicts the BS, you will find more and more evidence will start to present itself, like a snowball effect. Your job is to actively search for things that will make your unconscious mind question itself.

What inner rules or "limiting beliefs" are you living by? Are they serving you?

i.e.) You feel like moving is stressful... so you tell yourself you need to pack early so it won't be so stressful when it comes time. But you begin getting stressed because you feel you're not getting on it and packing soon enough. So, instead of stress later you're creating stress now. The inner rule you create can make the stress worse.

i.e.) Have you ever signed up for some type of event or seminar and then felt you didn't want to go? But you made yourself go anyway, because you felt you "had to" either because of the financial commitment, other's expectations, or you just feel it's what you're supposed to do. When you drive your choice based on your BS, going to this event feels like a punishment. Does the belief of "having to" really mean anything? Does it serve you?

Write some inner rules or limiting beliefs that you have:

Choosing Empowering Beliefs

There are a lot of outside influences that impact how we feel, what we do, and most of all, what we believe. There are common limiting belief systems that are passed from generation to generation and person to person much like a virus—a mind virus. These sneaky viruses usually go undetected because they are so common, or normal in our society, that one rarely even notices that they have been infected. For this reason, limiting BS are really easy to spread.

The good news is that there is an easy cure—awareness! Once you become aware of one of these little buggers, you can choose to believe something different, immediately killing the virus! Below, first become aware of which mind viruses you have and then *question* them. When we question a belief, we often find evidence to the contrary, which weakens our acceptance of it. When we weaken a belief, it's like knocking the legs out from under a table. It just can't stand anymore!

Common Limiting Beliefs:

"Money is the root of all evil."   *"Money doesn't grow on trees."*

"Don't burn your bridges."   *"No pain no gain."*

"Life is hard."   *"Good things come to those who wait."*

"You have to pay your dues."

Which of these phrases were you conditioned to believe?

Can you think of others?

Can you see any fears you developed because of them?

Can you see any way in which they have limited you?

Where did the idea come from? Are you sure it's true?

Who told you this? Are you sure they were right?

Do you have evidence that goes against these limiting beliefs?

Do you have evidence that affirms the empowering belief you WANT to have?

If you can't prove these limiting beliefs true beyond a reasonable doubt, can you discard them?

Belief Reflection Exercise

When looking back at your story and the important scenes, take notes of any beliefs you picked up along the way. Write down the beliefs you developed about the topics below and consider what other influential beliefs you may have acquired.

About yourself

About others

About your needs

About being an adult

About working and career

About relationships

About your roles

About how to succeed

About responsibility

About your value and worth

About control of your life

[ ]

About the purpose or goal of life

[ ]

About priorities

[ ]

OTHER BELIEFS

[ ]

Changing Your Beliefs

How would you choose to believe NOW? Go back through all the beliefs you wrote down and decide if you would change them, and if so, write a new belief below.

About yourself

[ ]

About others

[ ]

About your needs

[ ]

About being an adult

[ ]

About working and career

[ ]

About relationships

[ ]

About your roles

About how to succeed

About responsibility

About your value and worth

About control of your life

About the purpose or goal of life

About priorities

OTHER BELIEFS

Excuses: Say NO to But!

Replace your excuses with commitments!

Just as with the "mind viruses" mentioned previously, we all have common phrases we've picked up from our families and cultures that are nothing more than excuses. By becoming aware of them, questioning them, and changing the way we view the underlying fears behind them, we can change the way we think, and empower ourselves!

When you catch yourself saying "but..." it's a signal that you're about to make an excuse for why you're not living your life the way you want—on purpose! Catch yourself and rephrase your excuse into positive affirmation that will help you stay committed.

Which of the following common "buts" has held you back in the past?

____ But, it's too hard.　　　　　　　　____ But, it's too risky.

____ But, it'll take too long.　　　　　　____ But, it's overwhelming.

____ But, I don't have time.　　　　　　　____ Others

_____

_____
_____
_____
_____

_____

For each excuse you commonly use, write a positive affirmation statement. For example, change "I don't have time" to "I make time for what is important to me."

1.

2.

3.

4.

5.

6.

Take Your Power Back!

Most of us are operating on low power levels. Why? Because we give our power away. How? By allowing other people's actions and beliefs to affect us, and by directing our energy and attention toward negative things or toward other people. Your ability to live in alignment with your purpose will be amplified by taking your power back! Answer the questions below and evaluate how much power you give away—and then take it back!

Who or what do I blame for any negative situation?

In what way do I feel pressure to achieve? To please?

What % of my energy goes to:

Pleasing my family?	_____ %
Pleasing others?	_____ %
Being pessimistic?	_____ %
Thinking about resentment?	_____ %
Negative self-judgment?	_____ %
Regrets about failures?	_____ %
Controlling others/experiences?	_____ %
Worrying?	_____ %
My AUTHENTIC self?	_____ %

Make sure it adds up to 100%.

Now, take back your power! You cannot change the past, or live for others. Free yourself and you'll be amazed how much you can create in your life!

Clarifying Your Purpose

Now, it's time to look back over everything you've been working on and see how it all fits together. What trajectory do you see your life has been taking and where does it all seem to be pointing you? Below, write a brief summary of everything you've gone over. Seeing it all in one place is very powerful and clarifying.

After looking over the **influences from your childhood**, what do you feel is YOUR authentic world view and roles in this life?

After reviewing your **passions and interests**, which ones stand out as having the most meaning and being the most inspirational?

After considering your **talents and skills**, which do you feel are the most useful and purposeful?

Can you see how **coincidences** have played a role in your life? Where have they been leading you? If they've always been leading you down your true path, do you believe they always will?

What **turning points** have you experienced in your life that seem to have clearly pushed you toward a life of purpose and meaning?

What does it seem you were born to do?

What does it seem your life has been leading up to?

What do you seem to be in the business of doing?

What are the 3-5 MAIN points that stand out above the rest and summarize your main mission in life?

When you put the puzzle together, in one sentence, what does your purpose look like?

My purpose is to:

Writing Your Manifesto

Now that you have DISCOVERED YOUR PURPOSE and eliminated the limitations that have been holding you back, it's time to put your newfound mission out to the world, by writing your MANIFESTO! A manifesto is a declaration of your beliefs, opinions, motives, and intentions. You have your purpose, now you get to put into words WHY that's your purpose.

Your manifesto explains who you truly are and what you stand for. Many important figures throughout history, as well as inspirational companies today, use manifestos as a call to action to their Tribe—their ideal clients, their like-minded peers, their kindred spirits. You can use your manifesto to connect to your Tribe, but most importantly, your manifesto is meant to inspire YOU. There will be times in life where you feel out of alignment with your purpose. You may feel discouraged. You may lose that feeling of clarity and excitement about your journey. In those moments, you can revisit your manifesto, stir your passions, and rekindle your inspiration for following the path of purpose that your entire life has been leading you toward.

There is an example of Transformation's manifesto at the bottom of this activity.

My purpose is:

My top 3 personal core values:

Key phrases or quotes that capture my world view and point of view:

What are characteristics of people who would be part of your Tribe:

This is what I stand for:

This is WHY I want to fulfill my purpose:

Sample Manifesto:

The Transformation Academy Manifesto

When we were young, we blindly went where every man/woman has gone before...

To school, to get good grades, to go to college, to get a good job, to work until we're 65, retire, live in poverty for 5 - 10 years, and die.

We were unfulfilled and restless and lived life on autopilot. We did what we "should".

But we knew deeply, that life is meant to be more.

The status quo makes us gag.

We were not born to live in a box.

We were created to be free.

We are lifelong learners on a never-ending quest to reach our potential.

We think outside of our "but" (excuse) and question our B.S. (belief systems).

We're purpose-driven and heart-centered.

We came to this earth to use our gifts and make a difference.

We live life on our terms by taking radical, personal responsibility.

We turn pain into purpose and find the blessings in our challenges.

We are unstoppable, and we don't need permission to embrace our greatness.

It's not that we have no fear, it's that we do it anyway.

And, when we're not motivated, we dream bigger.

We are the masters of our destiny.

We are freedom junkies and time is our currency.

We believe entrepreneurship is the ultimate form of empowerment.

We work hard but play harder.

We will fulfill our purpose or die trying.

There is no plan b.

We run more than a business; we lead a movement.

We are a little bit crazy and wouldn't have it any other way.

We are authentically, totally, and emphatically us.

We own it. We don't apologize.

We are Transformation.

Now, it's time to write YOUR Manifesto!

Rewriting Your Life Story

Through our lives, beginning in childhood, we have experiences and influences that condition us to hold certain beliefs. These beliefs are then the basis on which we tell the story of who we are, to ourselves and to others. Our parents and caretakers influence us with their own beliefs, the stories they tell about life, and the way that they live. We then have our own experiences that either confirm what we've been taught or give us a varied perspective of life. We are domesticated into the societal norms of our culture, country, neighborhood, religion, and ethnicity. We are influenced by the media, the educational system, and our friends.

We are all natural story tellers, and so we automatically tell ourselves and others a story of who we are and how the world works. This story is told by default, based on the beliefs we picked up about our self and the world and our own personal experience. When we tell these stories, we are usually not aware. Even if we are aware, we often don't know why we tell what we tell, and the story is not necessarily based on fact.

Our life stories are more fiction than non-fiction, even though we often assume they are real.

Below is an activity called My Life Movie that will help you see what story you tell about your life, as well as give you an opportunity to rewrite your script. Then, in the Belief Reflection Exercise, you'll delve deeper into the beliefs that support the story you used to tell, and reflect on ways to change those beliefs and align to the NEW STORY you want to live.

Activity: My Life Movie

The purpose of the My Life Movie activity is to put your life and the things you wish to change into perspective. One of the main reasons that many people are unsatisfied in life and not living in alignment with their highest purpose, is because of the stories they tell themselves and others about their life and who they are. By viewing your own Life Movie, you will be able to see more clearly the story you are living and will then be able to rewrite your script!

You are the star in your own Life Movie! Your Life Movie is the vision you see in your mind of your life story, including your visions and dreams, your beliefs about life and who you are, and how you think about your past and future. Some scenes are memories from your life, and you often see these clips over and over in your mind.

What scenes from your past do you replay frequently (positive and negative)? These may be life changing events, pivotal moments, coincidental moments, etc.

What are your most influential or "climactic" scenes?

[blank box]

In a one paragraph review of Your Movie, please describe the "background story":

[blank box]

Other parts of Your Movie include the stories you tell yourself and others about who you are now. Is your story one of bravery and perseverance, leading you to your current state of success and fulfillment? Is your story one of being the victim of an unfortunate life in which you had bad luck, got the short end of the stick, or were mistreated by others? Or, is your story one of boredom and unfulfillment, letting fear or other people's opinions keep you from living the life of your dreams, one in which you find yourself existing instead of living?

In a one paragraph review of Your Movie, please describe the characteristics of the "main character" and the story of who they are:

[blank box]

Finally, Your Movie includes your vision, and stories about your future.

In a one paragraph review of Your Movie, please describe the "plot" including what will happen to the main character:

[blank box]

Two important things to know about Your Movie:

1. You are constantly, actively writing and directing your film.
2. Your Movie becomes Your Life.

Yes, you are the one who both writes your screen play and directs every scene. This includes the scenes from your past. "How," you might ask, "did I write the script for the ways I was mistreated as a child or the unfortunate circumstances that happened to me as an adult? I didn't have control over them, and I certainly would not have chosen them." You're right. But you do have the power to decide what to do now. What is important for you to know is that THE PAST HAPPENED, yes, but it is over – it no longer exists. The Movie scenes you play in your mind are simply memory traces in your brain. You are NOT your past. You are not a memory trace in your brain.

Your Movie and your story create the life you live, not the other way around. If you tell yourself or others that you are a certain way, you will act accordingly. If you tell yourself or others that certain things are going to happen to you, they will. You can look at it from a spiritual perspective – that what you focus your attention on you will attract to your life (The Law of Attraction), or you can look at it from a psychological perspective – if you believe something will happen you will unconsciously do things that will cause it to happen (Self-Fulfilling Prophecy). Either way, this is the reality of life.

Who else do you let write scenes in your script? Are there things you believe and do because others (like your parents) said you "should"?

```

```

Is your story the one you want to be telling? If not, what would you change?

```

```

Can you see any ways that telling your story limits you?

```

```

Now it is time for you to re-write Your Life Movie!

(You can do this now or wait until after you complete the Belief Reflection Exercise below.)

In a one paragraph review of Your Movie, please describe the "background story" you WANT to tell:

In a one paragraph review of Your Movie, please describe the characteristics you want the "main character" to have and the story of who they want to be:

In a one paragraph review of Your Movie, please describe the "plot" including what you want to happen to the main character:

For other workbooks and the online courses that accompany them,
visit www.transformationacademy.com.

Made in the USA
Las Vegas, NV
17 June 2024

91137075R00022